easy

Curries

easy

Curries

Love Food ® is an imprint of Parragon Books Ltd

Parragon
Queen Street House
4 Queen Street
Bath BA1 1HE, UK

Designed by Mark Cavanagh
Additional photography by Clive Bozzard-Hill
Additional Food styling by Sandra Baddeley
Introduction by Anne Sheasby

ISBN: 978-1-4075-2356-9
Printed in China

NOTES FOR THE READER
• This book uses imperial, metric, and US cup measurements. Follow the same units of measurement
throughout; do not mix imperial and metric.
• All spoon measurements are level: teaspoons are assumed to be 5 ml, and tablespoons are assumed
to be 15 ml.
• Unless otherwise stated, milk is assumed to be lowfat and eggs are medium. The times given are an
approximate guide only.
• Some recipes contain nuts. If you are allergic to nuts you should avoid using them and any products
containing nuts.
• Recipes using raw or very lightly cooked eggs should be avoided by infants, the elderly, pregnant
women, convalescents, and anyone suffering from illness.

Contents

	Introduction	6
1	Poultry & Meat	10
2	Fish & Seafood	48
3	Vegetable Dishes	86
4	Accompaniments	124
	Index	160

Introduction

Curries are associated with many Asian countries including India, Bangladesh, Pakistan, Sri Lanka, Thailand, Indonesia, and Malaysia. Some other regions around the globe, such as South Africa, the Caribbean, Singapore, and Vietnam, also have their own versions of curry-based dishes.

Over the centuries, curries have become a popular choice in many countries worldwide. Today there are many great establishments producing and serving excellent curry dishes, but, as this cookbook demonstrates, curries are quick and easy to make at home. By combining a selection of fresh ingredients and spices, you will soon be creating tempting curries in your own kitchen.

Origins of Curry

It is believed that the term "curry" originates from the Tamil word "kari" which means "spiced sauce". Originally the word curry referred to a combination of ingredients stewed together with liquid and various spices to create a sauce or type of casserole. These days, partly owing to its migration to many regions of the world, curry has now taken on a wider meaning. Generally speaking, the term curry now denotes a variety of dishes comprising a combination of ingredients cooked together to create a range of savory, often sauce-based dishes, all of which are spiced.

Curries vary from one region to another—some are creamy and mild, such as Korma, others, such as Madras, tend to be medium-hot, while curries like Vindaloo are the really hot and spicy ones.

To complete the meal, curries are often served with a range of appetizing accompaniments including naan bread, chapatis, pilau rice, mango chutney, lime pickle, raita, and so on. Again, the selection of accompaniments will vary according to the choice of the main dish.

Spices

A combination of spices, usually in the form of ground spices or a spice paste, is an essential component of a curry. Ready-made powders and pastes are widely available, but it is preferable to buy whole, dried spices and grind or crush them yourself at home, as required.

A clean electric coffee grinder (kept specifically for spices) is an ideal way to grind your own spices. Alternatively, a pestle and mortar can be used. You will find that grinding or crushing your own spices will bring out their lovely aromatic flavors and will vastly improve the taste of your dishes. Try dry-frying whole spices in a heavy skillet over moderate heat for a few minutes before grinding them—this will help to bring out their flavors even more.

The blend of spices used to make a basic curry powder or paste varies enormously from region to region, but spices commonly used in curry-making include coriander, cumin, fenugreek and mustard seeds, black peppercorns, turmeric, chiles, cardamom, cinnamon, cloves, and sometimes ground ginger. It very much depends on personal taste and how hot you like your curry to be, so choose a mixture of spices that suits your palate best.

Storing Spices

It is best to buy whole spices in small quantities to be sure that they remain as fresh as possible. Once freshly ground to a fine powder, spice mixtures should keep well in an airtight container for up to a month. However, ground spices do deteriorate quite quickly so, if possible, it is best to grind spices freshly each time you cook.

If you do buy ready-ground spices, make sure that you store them in a cool, dark, dry place and preferably not in glass jars in a spice rack on the kitchen wall—this may look attractive but it is probably the worst way to store dried spices!

Other Ingredients

Other ingredients such as onions, tomatoes, garlic, fresh ginger, coconut, tamarind, and fresh cilantro play an important role in many curries. Chiles, both fresh and dried, are also an essential ingredient in numerous curry dishes.

The majority of chiles are green when they are unripe (or immature) and they then ripen to varying shades of red. The color of a fresh chile is not an indication of how hot the flavor of the chile will be. As a general rule, the smaller and thinner the chile, the hotter it will be. You can reduce the heat of a fresh chile by cutting it in half lengthwise and scraping out the seeds and core (or membranes) before use.

When preparing fresh chiles, it is a good idea to wear disposable gloves, as the natural oils in chiles may cause irritation to your skin and eyes. If you don't have any gloves, make sure you wash your hands thoroughly after preparing chiles.

Thai Red Curry Paste

1 tbsp coriander seeds

1 tbsp cumin seeds

2 tsp shrimp paste

12 dried or fresh red chiles, chopped

2 shallots, chopped

8 garlic cloves, chopped

1-inch/2.5-cm piece of fresh galangal, chopped

2 lemongrass stalks (white part only), chopped

4 kaffir lime leaves, chopped

2 tbsp chopped cilantro root

grated rind of 1 lime

1 tsp black peppercorns

Dry-fry the coriander and cumin seeds in a heavy-bottom skillet, stirring constantly, for 2–3 minutes, until browned. Remove from the heat and grind to a powder with a mortar and pestle or spice grinder, or process in a blender. Wrap the shrimp paste in a piece of foil and broil or dry-fry for 2–3 minutes, turning once or twice.

Put the ground spices, shrimp paste, and chiles into a blender or food processor and process until finely chopped. Add the remaining ingredients and process again to a smooth paste, scraping down the sides as necessary.

Thai Green Curry Paste

Follow the instructions for Thai Red Curry Paste, but replace the chiles with 15 fresh green Thai chiles, use only 6 garlic cloves, increase the number of kaffir lime leaves to 6, and add 1 teaspoon of salt with the pepper.

Thai Yellow Curry Paste

3 small fresh orange or yellow chiles, coarsely chopped

3 large garlic cloves, coarsely chopped

4 shallots, coarsely chopped

3 tsp ground turmeric

1 tsp salt

12–15 black peppercorns

1 lemongrass stalk (white part only), coarsely chopped

1-inch/2.5-cm piece fresh ginger, chopped

Put all the ingredients in a food processor or blender and process to a thick paste, scraping down the sides as necessary.

Mussaman Curry Paste

4 large dried red chiles

2 tsp shrimp paste

3 shallots, finely chopped

3 garlic cloves, finely chopped

1-inch/2.5-cm piece fresh galangal, finely chopped

2 lemongrass stalks (white part only), finely chopped

2 cloves

1 tbsp coriander seeds

1 tbsp cumin seeds

seeds from 3 cardamom pods

1 tsp black peppercorns

1 tsp salt

Place the chiles in a bowl, cover with hot water and set aside to soak for 30–45 minutes. Wrap the shrimp paste in aluminum foil and broil or dry-fry in a skillet for 2–3 minutes, turning once or twice. Remove from the broiler or skillet. Dry-fry the shallots, garlic, galangal, lemon grass, cloves, coriander, cumin, and cardamom seeds over a low heat, stirring frequently, for 3–4 minutes until lightly browned. Transfer to a food processor and process until finely ground. Add the chiles and their soaking liquid, peppercorns and salt and process again. Add the shrimp paste and process again to a smooth paste, scraping down the sides as necessary.

Garlic & Ginger Paste

Blend together equal quantities of garlic and fresh ginger. Store in a sealed jar in the refrigerator for up to 3 weeks, or in a freezer for up to 1 month.

Poultry & Meat

Chicken Tikka Masala

serves 4–6

1 oz/30 g ghee or 2 tbsp vegetable or groundnut oil

1 large garlic clove, finely chopped

1 fresh red chile, seeded and chopped

2 tsp ground cumin

2 tsp paprika

14 oz/400 g canned chopped tomatoes

10 fl oz/300 ml heavy cream

8 pieces cooked tandoori chicken

salt and pepper

sprigs of fresh cilantro, to garnish

To make the tikka masala, heat the ghee in a large skillet with a lid over medium heat. Add the garlic and chile and stir-fry for 1 minute. Stir in the cumin, paprika, and salt and pepper to taste and continue stirring for about 30 seconds.

Stir the tomatoes with their juice and the cream into the pan. Reduce the heat to low and let the sauce simmer for about 10 minutes, stirring frequently, until it reduces and thickens.

Meanwhile, remove all the bones and any skin from the tandoori chicken pieces, then cut the meat into bite-size pieces.

Adjust the seasoning of the sauce, if necessary. Add the chicken pieces to the pan, cover, and let simmer for 3–5 minutes until the chicken is heated through. Sprinkle with the cilantro sprigs.

Chicken Korma

serves 4

1 chicken, weighing 3 lb/
1.3 kg

1 cup butter

3 onions, thinly sliced

1 garlic clove, crushed

1-inch/2.5-cm piece fresh
ginger, grated

1 tsp mild chili powder

1 tsp ground turmeric

1 tsp ground coriander

½ tsp ground cardamom

½ tsp ground cinnamon

½ tsp salt

1 tbsp chickpea flour

½ cup milk

2 cups heavy cream

fresh cilantro leaves,
to garnish

freshly cooked rice,
to serve

Put the chicken into a large pan, cover with water, and bring to a boil. Reduce the heat, cover, and simmer for 30 minutes. Remove from the heat, lift out the chicken, and set aside to cool. Reserve ½ cup of the cooking liquid. Remove and discard the skin and bones. Cut the flesh into bite-size pieces.

Heat the butter in a large pan over medium heat. Add the onions and garlic and cook, stirring, for 3 minutes, or until softened. Add the ginger, chili powder, turmeric, ground coriander, cardamom, cinnamon, and salt and cook for a further 5 minutes. Add the chicken and the reserved cooking liquid. Cook for 2 minutes.

Blend the chickpea flour with a little of the milk and add to the pan, then stir in the remaining milk. Bring to a boil, stirring, then reduce the heat, cover, and simmer for 25 minutes. Stir in the cream, cover, and simmer for a further 15 minutes.

Garnish with cilantro leaves and serve with freshly cooked rice.

Chicken Jalfrezi

serves 4

½ tsp cumin seeds

½ tsp coriander seeds

1 tsp mustard oil

3 tbsp vegetable oil

1 large onion, finely chopped

3 garlic cloves, crushed

1 tbsp tomato paste

2 tomatoes, peeled and chopped

1 tsp ground turmeric

½ tsp chili powder

½ tsp garam masala

1 tsp red wine vinegar

1 small red bell pepper, seeded and chopped

4½ oz/125 g frozen fava beans

1 lb 2 oz/500 g cooked chicken, chopped

salt

fresh cilantro sprigs, to garnish

freshly cooked rice, to serve

Grind the cumin and coriander seeds in a mortar with a pestle, then reserve. Heat the mustard oil in a large, heavy-bottom skillet over high heat for 1 minute, or until it begins to smoke. Add the vegetable oil, reduce the heat, and add the onion and garlic. Cook for 10 minutes, or until golden.

Add the tomato paste, tomatoes, turmeric, chili powder, garam masala, vinegar, reserved ground cumin, and coriander seeds to the skillet. Stir the mixture until fragrant.

Add the red bell pepper and fava beans and stir for an additional 2 minutes, or until the bell pepper is softened. Stir in the chicken, and season to taste with salt, then simmer gently for 6–8 minutes, until the chicken is heated through and the beans are tender. Transfer to warmed serving dishes, garnish with sprigs of cilantro, and serve with freshly cooked rice.

Thai Green Chicken Curry

serves 4

2 tbsp peanut or corn oil

2 tbsp Thai Green Curry Paste

1 lb 2 oz/500 g skinless, boneless chicken breasts, cut into cubes

2 kaffir lime leaves, roughly torn

1 lemongrass stalk, finely chopped

1 cup coconut milk

16 baby eggplants, halved

2 tbsp Thai fish sauce

sprigs of fresh Thai basil and thinly sliced kaffir lime leaves, to garnish

Heat the oil in a preheated wok or large, heavy-bottom skillet. Add the curry paste and stir-fry briefly until all the aromas are released.

Add the chicken, lime leaves, and lemongrass and stir-fry for 3–4 minutes, until the meat is beginning to color. Add the coconut milk and eggplants and simmer gently for 8–10 minutes, or until tender.

Stir in the fish sauce and serve immediately garnished with sprigs of Thai basil and lime leaves.

Balti Chicken

serves 6

3 tbsp ghee or vegetable oil

2 large onions, sliced

3 tomatoes, sliced

½ tsp nigella seeds

4 black peppercorns

2 cardamom pods

1 cinnamon stick

1 tsp chili powder

1 tsp garam masala

2 tsp Garlic and Ginger Paste

1 lb 9 oz/700 g skinless, boneless chicken breasts or thighs, diced

2 tbsp plain yogurt

2 tbsp chopped fresh cilantro, plus extra sprigs to garnish

2 fresh green chiles, seeded and finely chopped

2 tbsp lime juice

salt

Heat the ghee in a large, heavy-bottom skillet. Add the onions and cook over low heat, stirring occasionally, for 10 minutes, or until golden. Add the tomatoes, nigella seeds, peppercorns, cardamom pods, cinnamon stick, chili powder, garam masala, garlic and ginger paste, and season to taste with salt. Cook, stirring constantly, for 5 minutes.

Add the chicken and cook, stirring constantly, for 5 minutes, or until well coated in the spice paste. Stir in the yogurt. Cover and let simmer, stirring occasionally, for 10 minutes.

Stir in the chopped cilantro, chiles, and lime juice. Transfer to a warmed serving dish, garnish with sprigs of cilantro, and serve immediately.

Lamb Rogan Josh

serves 4

1½ cups plain yogurt

½ tsp ground asafetida dissolved in 2 tbsp water

1 lb 9 oz/700 g boneless leg of lamb, trimmed and cut into 2-inch/5-cm cubes

2 tomatoes, seeded and chopped

1 onion, chopped

2 tbsp ghee or vegetable or peanut oil

1½ tbsp Garlic & Ginger Paste

2 tbsp tomato paste

2 bay leaves

1 tbsp ground coriander

¼–1 tsp chili powder, ideally Kashmiri chili powder

½ tsp ground turmeric

1 tsp salt

½ tsp garam masala

Put the yogurt in a large bowl and stir in the dissolved asafetida. Add the lamb and use your hands to rub in all the marinade, then set aside for 30 minutes.

Meanwhile, put the tomatoes and onion in a food processor or blender and process until blended. Heat the ghee in a flameproof casserole or large skillet with a tight-fitting lid. Add the garlic and ginger paste and stir around until the aromas are released.

Stir in the tomato mixture, tomato paste, bay leaves, coriander, chili powder, and turmeric, reduce the heat to low, and simmer, stirring occasionally, for 5–8 minutes.

Add the lamb and salt with any leftover marinade and stir around for 2 minutes. Cover, reduce the heat to low, and simmer, stirring occasionally, for 30 minutes. The lamb should give off enough moisture to prevent it catching on the bottom of the pan, but if the sauce looks too dry, stir in a little water.

Sprinkle the lamb with the garam masala, re-cover the pan, and continue simmering for 15–20 minutes until the lamb is tender. Serve immediately.

Lamb, Tomato & Eggplant Curry

serves 4

2 tbsp oil

1 lb 2 oz/500 g lamb fillet or leg, cut into cubes

1 large onion, coarsely chopped

2–3 tbsp Thai Red Curry Paste

1 eggplant, cut into small cubes

10 tomatoes, peeled, seeded, and coarsely chopped

1¾ cups coconut milk

1¼ cups lamb stock

2 tbsp chopped fresh cilantro, plus extra sprigs to garnish

Heat the oil in a large skillet. Add the lamb in batches and cook for 8–10 minutes, or until browned all over. Remove with a slotted spoon and set aside.

Add the onion to the skillet and cook for 2–3 minutes, or until just softened. Add the curry paste and stir-fry for an additional 2 minutes. Add the eggplant, three-quarters of the tomatoes, and the lamb and stir together.

Add the coconut milk and stock and let simmer gently for 30–40 minutes, until the lamb is tender and the curry has thickened.

Mix the remaining tomatoes and chopped cilantro together in a small bowl, then stir into the curry. Serve immediately, garnished with cilantro sprigs.

Lamb Do Piaza

serves 4

4 onions, sliced into rings

3 garlic cloves, coarsely chopped

1-inch/2.5-cm piece fresh ginger, grated

1 tsp ground coriander

1 tsp ground cumin

1 tsp chili powder

½ tsp ground turmeric

1 tsp ground cinnamon

1 tsp garam masala

4 tbsp water

5 tbsp butter or vegetable oil

1 lb 8 oz/680 g boneless lamb, cut into bite-size chunks

6 tbsp plain yogurt

salt and pepper

fresh cilantro leaves, to garnish

freshly cooked rice, to serve

Put half of the onion rings into a food processor with the garlic, ginger, ground coriander, cumin, chili powder, turmeric, cinnamon, and garam masala. Add the water and process to a paste.

Heat 4 tablespoons of the butter in a pan over medium heat. Add the remaining onions and cook, stirring, for 3 minutes. Remove from the heat. Lift out the onions with a slotted spoon and set aside. Heat the remaining butter in the pan over high heat, add the lamb, and cook, stirring, for 5 minutes. Lift out the meat and drain on paper towels.

Add the onion paste to the pan and cook over medium heat, stirring, until the oil separates. Stir in the yogurt, season to taste with salt and pepper, return the lamb to the pan, and stir well.

Bring the mixture gently to a boil, reduce the heat, cover, and simmer for 25 minutes. Stir in the reserved onion rings and cook for a further 5 minutes. Remove from the heat, and garnish with cilantro leaves. Serve immediately with freshly cooked rice.

Lamb Pasanda

serves 4–6

1 lb 5 oz/600 g boneless shoulder or leg of lamb

2 tbsp Garlic & Ginger Paste

4 tbsp ghee or vegetable or peanut oil

3 large onions, chopped

1 fresh green chile, seeded and chopped

2 green cardamom pods, lightly crushed

1 cinnamon stick, broken in half

2 tsp ground coriander

1 tsp ground cumin

1 tsp ground turmeric

generous 1 cup water

2/3 cup heavy cream

4 tbsp ground almonds

1½ tsp salt

1 tsp garam masala

paprika and toasted slivered almonds, to garnish

freshly cooked rice, to serve

Cut the meat into thin slices, then place the slices between plastic wrap and pound with a rolling pin or meat mallet to make them even thinner. Put the lamb slices in a bowl, add the garlic and ginger paste, and use your hands to rub the paste into the lamb. Cover and set aside in a cool place to marinate for 2 hours.

Heat the ghee in a large skillet with a tight-fitting lid over medium–high heat. Add the onions and chile and sauté, stirring frequently, for 5–8 minutes until the onions are golden brown.

Stir in the cardamom pods, cinnamon stick, coriander, cumin, and turmeric and continue stirring for 2 minutes, or until the spices are aromatic.

Add the meat to the pan and cook, stirring occasionally, for about 5 minutes until it is brown on all sides and the fat begins to separate. Stir in the water and bring to a boil, still stirring. Reduce the heat to its lowest setting, cover the pan tightly, and simmer for 40 minutes, or until the meat is tender.

When the lamb is tender, stir the cream and ground almonds together in a bowl. Beat in 6 tablespoons of the hot cooking liquid from the pan, then gradually beat this mixture back into the pan. Stir in the salt and garam masala. Continue to simmer for an additional 5 minutes, uncovered, stirring occasionally.

Garnish with a sprinkling of paprika and toasted slivered almonds and serve with freshly cooked rice.

Lean Lamb Cooked in Spinach

serves 2–4

1¼ cups vegetable oil

2 onions, sliced

¼ bunch of fresh cilantro

2 fresh green chiles, chopped

1½ tsp finely chopped fresh ginger

1½ tsp crushed fresh garlic

1 tsp chili powder

½ tsp ground turmeric

1 lb/450 g lean lamb, cut into bite-size chunks

1 tsp salt

2 lb 4 oz/1 kg fresh spinach, trimmed, washed, and chopped

3 cups water

1 fresh red chile, finely chopped, to garnish

Heat the oil in a large, heavy-bottom skillet. Add the onions and cook until light golden.

Add the fresh cilantro and green chiles to the skillet and stir-fry for 3–5 minutes. Reduce the heat and add the ginger, garlic, chili powder, and turmeric, stirring well.

Add the lamb to the skillet and stir-fry for an additional 5 minutes. Add the salt and the spinach and cook, stirring occasionally with a wooden spoon, for an additional 3–5 minutes.

Add the water, stirring, and cook over low heat, covered, for 45 minutes. Remove the lid and check the meat. If it is not tender, turn the meat over, increase the heat, and cook, uncovered, until the surplus water has been absorbed. Stir-fry the mixture for an additional 5–7 minutes.

Transfer the lamb and spinach mixture to a warmed serving dish and garnish with chopped red chile. Serve hot.

Pork with Cinnamon & Fenugreek

serves 4

1 tsp ground coriander

1 tsp ground cumin

1 tsp chili powder

1 tbsp dried fenugreek leaves (methi)

1 tsp ground fenugreek

⅔ cup plain yogurt

1 lb/450 g diced pork tenderloin

4 tbsp ghee or vegetable oil

1 large onion, sliced

2-inch/5-cm piece fresh ginger, finely chopped

4 garlic cloves, finely chopped

1 cinnamon stick

6 cardamom pods

6 whole cloves

2 bay leaves

¾ cup water

salt

Mix the coriander, cumin, chili powder, dried fenugreek, ground fenugreek, and yogurt together in a small bowl. Place the pork in a large, shallow, nonmetallic dish and add the spice mixture, turning well to coat. Cover with plastic wrap and let marinate in the refrigerator for 30 minutes.

Heat the ghee in a large, heavy-bottom pan. Cook the onion over low heat, stirring occasionally, for 5 minutes, or until softened. Add the ginger, garlic, cinnamon stick, cardamom pods, cloves, and bay leaves and cook, stirring constantly, for 2 minutes, or until the spices give off their aroma. Add the meat with its marinade and the water, and season to taste with salt. Bring to a boil, reduce the heat, cover, and let simmer for 30 minutes.

Transfer the meat mixture to a preheated wok or large, heavy-bottom skillet and cook over low heat, stirring constantly, until dry and tender. If necessary, occasionally sprinkle with a little water to prevent it sticking to the wok. Serve immediately.

Red Curry with Pork

serves 4

2 tbsp vegetable or peanut oil

1 onion, coarsely chopped

2 garlic cloves, chopped

1 lb/450 g pork tenderloin, thickly sliced

1 red bell pepper, seeded and cut into squares

6 oz/175 g button mushrooms, quartered

2 tbsp Thai Red Curry Paste

2½ cups coconut cream

1 tsp pork or vegetable bouillon powder

2 tbsp Thai soy sauce

4 tomatoes, peeled, seeded, and chopped

handful of fresh cilantro, chopped

Heat the oil in a wok or large skillet and sauté the onion and garlic for 1–2 minutes, until they are softened but not browned.

Add the pork slices and stir-fry for 2–3 minutes until browned all over. Add the bell pepper, mushrooms, and curry paste.

Add the coconut cream to the wok with the bouillon powder and soy sauce. Bring to a boil and let simmer for 4–5 minutes until the liquid has reduced and thickened.

Add the tomatoes and cilantro and cook for 1–2 minutes before serving.

Pork Vindaloo

serves 4–6

4 tbsp mustard oil

2 large onions, finely chopped

6 bay leaves

6 cloves

6 garlic cloves, chopped

3 green cardamom pods, lightly cracked

1–2 small fresh red chiles, chopped

2 tbsp ground cumin

½ tsp salt

½ tsp ground turmeric

2 tbsp cider vinegar

2 tbsp water

1 tbsp tomato paste

1 lb 9 oz/700 g boneless shoulder of pork, trimmed and cut into 2-inch/5-cm cubes

Put the mustard oil in a large skillet or pan with a tight-fitting lid over high heat until it smokes. Turn off the heat and let the mustard oil cool completely.

Reheat the oil over medium–high heat. Add the onions and sauté, stirring frequently, for 5–8 minutes until soft but not colored.

Add the bay leaves, cloves, garlic, cardamom pods, chiles, cumin, salt, turmeric, and 1 tablespoon of the vinegar to the onions and stir around. Stir in the water, then cover the pan and simmer for about 1 minute, or until the water is absorbed and the fat separates.

Dissolve the tomato paste in the remaining vinegar, then stir it into the pan. Add the pork and stir around.

Add just enough water to cover the pork and bring to a boil. Reduce the heat to its lowest level, cover the pan tightly, and simmer for 40–60 minutes until the pork is tender.

If too much liquid remains in the pan when the pork is tender, use a slotted spoon to remove the pork from the pan and boil the liquid until it reduces to the required amount. Return the pork to the pan to heat through, then transfer to warmed serving dishes and serve.

Beef Madras

serves 4–6

1–2 dried red chiles

2 tsp ground coriander

2 tsp ground turmeric

1 tsp black mustard seeds

½ tsp ground ginger

¼ tsp ground pepper

5 oz/140 g creamed
coconut, grated and
dissolved in 1¼ cups
boiling water

4 tbsp ghee or vegetable or
peanut oil

2 onions, chopped

3 large garlic cloves,
chopped

1 lb 9 oz/700 g lean stewing
steak, trimmed and cut
into 2-inch/5-cm cubes

generous 1 cup beef stock

lemon juice

salt

sprigs of fresh cilantro,
to garnish

freshly cooked rice,
to serve

Depending on how hot you want this dish to be, chop the chiles with or without any seeds. The more seeds you include, the hotter the dish will be. Put the chopped chile and any seeds in a small bowl with the ground coriander, turmeric, mustard seeds, ginger, and pepper and stir in a little of the coconut mixture to make a thin paste.

Heat the ghee in a large skillet with a tight-fitting lid over medium-high heat. Add the onions and garlic and sauté for 5–8 minutes, stirring frequently, until the onion is golden brown. Add the spice paste and stir around for 2 minutes, or until the aromas are released.

Add the meat and stock and bring to a boil. Reduce the heat to its lowest level, cover tightly, and simmer for 90 minutes, or until the beef is tender. Check occasionally that the meat isn't catching on the bottom of the pan and stir in a little extra water or stock, if necessary.

Uncover the pan and stir in the remaining coconut milk with the lemon juice and salt to taste. Bring to a boil, stirring, then reduce the heat again and simmer, still uncovered, until the sauce reduces slightly. Garnish with sprigs of coriander and serve with freshly cooked rice.

Balti Beef Curry

serves 4

2 tbsp ghee or vegetable oil

1 onion, thinly sliced

1 garlic clove, finely chopped

1¼-inch/3-cm piece fresh ginger, grated

2 fresh red chiles, seeded and finely chopped

1 lb/450 g rump steak, cut into thin strips

1 green bell pepper, seeded and thinly sliced

1 yellow bell pepper, seeded and thinly sliced

1 tsp ground cumin

1 tbsp garam masala

4 tomatoes, chopped

2 tbsp lemon juice

1 tbsp water

salt

chopped fresh cilantro, to garnish

Heat 1 tablespoon of the ghee in a preheated wok or large, heavy-bottom skillet. Add the onion and cook over low heat, stirring occasionally, for 8–10 minutes, or until golden. Increase the heat to medium, add the garlic, ginger, chiles, and steak and cook, stirring occasionally, for 5 minutes, or until the steak is browned all over. Remove with a slotted spoon and keep warm.

Add the remaining ghee to the wok, add the bell peppers and cook over medium heat, stirring occasionally, for 4 minutes, or until softened. Stir in the cumin and garam masala and cook, stirring, for 1 minute.

Add the tomatoes, lemon juice, and water, season to taste with salt and let simmer, stirring constantly, for 3 minutes. Return the steak mixture to the wok and heat through. Transfer to a warmed serving dish, garnish with cilantro and serve immediately.

Coconut Beef Curry

serves 4

1 tbsp ground coriander

1 tbsp ground cumin

3 tbsp Mussaman Curry Paste

scant 1 cup coconut cream

1 lb/450 g beef tenderloin,
cut into strips

1¾ cups coconut milk

½ cup unsalted peanuts,
finely chopped

2 tbsp fish sauce

1 tsp jaggery or soft light
brown sugar

4 kaffir lime leaves

Combine the coriander, cumin, and curry paste in a bowl.
Pour the coconut cream into a pan and bring just to a boil.
Add the curry paste mixture and let simmer for 1 minute.

Add the beef and let simmer for 6–8 minutes, then
add the coconut milk, peanuts, fish sauce, and sugar. Let
simmer gently for 15–20 minutes, until the meat is tender.

Add the lime leaves and let simmer for 1–2 minutes.
Serve hot.

Beef Korma with Almonds

serves 6

1¼ cups vegetable oil

3 onions, finely chopped

2 lb 4 oz/1 kg lean beef, cubed

1½ tsp garam masala

1½ tsp ground coriander

1½ tsp finely chopped fresh ginger

1½ tsp crushed fresh garlic

1 tsp salt

⅔ cup plain yogurt

2 whole cloves

3 green cardamom pods

4 black peppercorns

2½ cups water

Chapatis, to serve

to garnish

chopped blanched almonds

sliced fresh green chiles

chopped fresh cilantro

Heat the oil in a large, heavy-bottom skillet. Add the onions and stir-fry for 8–10 minutes, until golden. Remove half of the onions and set aside.

Add the meat to the remaining onions in the skillet and stir-fry for 5 minutes. Remove the skillet from the heat. Mix the garam masala, ground coriander, ginger, garlic, salt, and yogurt together in a large bowl. Gradually add the meat to the yogurt and spice mixture and mix to coat the meat on all sides. Place the meat mixture in the skillet, return to the heat, and stir-fry for 5–7 minutes, or until the mixture is nearly brown.

Add the cloves, cardamoms pods, and peppercorns. Add the water, reduce the heat, cover, and let simmer for 45–60 minutes. If the water has completely evaporated but the meat is still not tender enough, add another 1¼ cups water and cook for an additional 10–15 minutes, stirring occasionally. Transfer to warmed serving dishes and garnish with the reserved onions, chopped almonds, chiles and fresh coriander. Serve with chapatis.

Beef Dhansak

serves 6

2 tbsp ghee or vegetable oil

2 onions, chopped

3 garlic cloves, finely chopped

2 tsp ground coriander

2 ground cumin

2 tsp garam masala

1 tsp ground turmeric

1 lb/450 g zucchini, peeled and chopped, or bitter gourd or pumpkin, peeled, seeded, and chopped

1 eggplant, peeled and chopped

4 curry leaves

generous 1 cup masoor dal

4 cups water

2 lb 4 oz/1 kg stewing or braising steak, diced

salt

fresh cilantro leaves, to garnish

Heat the ghee in a large, heavy-bottom pan. Add the onions and garlic and cook over low heat, stirring occasionally, for 8–10 minutes, or until light golden. Stir in the ground coriander, cumin, garam masala, and turmeric and cook, stirring constantly, for 2 minutes.

Add the zucchini, eggplant, curry leaves, masoor dal, and water. Bring to a boil, then reduce the heat, cover, and let simmer for 30 minutes, or until the vegetables are tender. Remove the pan from the heat and let cool slightly. Transfer the mixture to a food processor, in batches if necessary, and process until smooth. Return the mixture to the pan and season to taste with salt.

Add the steak to the pan and bring to a boil. Reduce the heat, cover, and let simmer for 1¼ hours. Remove the lid and continue to simmer for an additional 30 minutes, or until the sauce is thick and the steak is tender. Serve garnished with cilantro leaves.

Fish &
Seafood

Mixed Seafood Curry

serves 4

1 tbsp vegetable or peanut oil

3 shallots, chopped finely

1-inch/2.5-cm piece fresh galangal, peeled and thinly sliced

2 garlic cloves, finely chopped

1¾ cups coconut milk

2 lemongrass stalks, snapped in half

4 tbsp Thai fish sauce

2 tbsp chili sauce

8 oz/225 g uncooked jumbo shrimp, peeled and deveined

8 oz/225 g baby squid, cleaned and thickly sliced

8 oz/225 g salmon fillet, skinned and cut into chunks

6 oz/175 g tuna steak, cut into chunks

8 oz/225 g fresh mussels, scrubbed and debearded

fresh Chinese chives, to garnish

freshly cooked rice, to serve

Heat the oil in a large wok with a tight-fitting lid and stir-fry the shallots, galangal, and garlic for 1–2 minutes, until they start to soften. Add the coconut milk, lemongrass, fish sauce, and chili sauce. Bring to a boil, reduce the heat, and let simmer for 1–2 minutes.

Add the shrimp, squid, salmon, and tuna, and let simmer for 3–4 minutes, until the shrimp have turned pink and the fish is cooked.

Discard any mussels with broken shells or any that refuse to close when tapped with a knife. Add the remaining mussels to the wok and cover with a lid. Let simmer for 1–2 minutes, until they have opened. Discard any mussels that remain closed. Garnish with Chinese chives and serve immediately with freshly cooked rice.

Fish Curry with Rice Noodles

serves 4

2 tbsp vegetable or peanut oil

1 large onion, chopped

2 garlic cloves, chopped

3 oz white mushrooms

8 oz/225 g monkfish, cut into cubes, each about 1 inch

8 oz/225 g salmon fillets, cut into 1-inch/2.5-cm cubes

8 oz/225 g cod, cut into 1-inch/2.5-cm cubes

2 tbsp Thai Red Curry Paste

1¾ cups coconut milk

handful of fresh cilantro, chopped, plus extra to garnish

1 tsp jaggery or soft light brown sugar

1 tsp Thai fish sauce

4 oz/115 g rice noodles

3 scallions, chopped

½ cup bean sprouts

a few fresh Thai basil leaves

Heat the oil in a wok or large skillet and gently sauté the onion, garlic, and mushrooms until softened but not browned.

Add the fish, curry paste, and coconut milk and bring gently to a boil. Let simmer for 2–3 minutes before adding the cilantro, jaggery, and fish sauce. Keep warm.

Meanwhile, soak the noodles for 3–4 minutes (or according to the package instructions) until tender, and drain well through a colander. Put the colander and noodles over a pan of simmering water. Add the scallions, bean sprouts, and basil and steam on top of the noodles for 1–2 minutes or until just wilted.

Pile the noodles onto warmed serving dishes and top with the fish curry. Sprinkle the remaining cilantro and basil over the top and serve immediately.

Fish in Coconut Milk

serves 4

2 tbsp vegetable or peanut oil

6 scallions, coarsely chopped

1-inch/2.5-cm piece fresh ginger, grated

2–3 tbsp Thai Red Curry Paste

1¾ cups coconut milk

⅔ cup fish stock

4 kaffir lime leaves

1 lemongrass stalk, broken in half

12 oz/350 g white fish fillets, skinned and cut into chunks

8 oz/225 g squid rings and tentacles

8 oz/225 g large cooked peeled shrimp

1 tbsp fish sauce

2 tbsp Thai soy sauce

4 tbsp snipped fresh Chinese chives

Heat the oil in a wok or large skillet and stir-fry the scallions and ginger for 1–2 minutes. Add the curry paste and stir-fry for 1–2 minutes.

Add the coconut milk, fish stock, lime leaves, and lemongrass. Bring to a boil, then reduce the heat and let simmer for 1 minute.

Add the fish, squid, and shrimp, and let simmer for 2–3 minutes, until the fish is cooked. Add the fish and soy sauces and stir in the chives. Serve immediately.

Goan-Style Seafood Curry

serves 4–6

3 tbsp vegetable or peanut oil

1 tbsp black mustard seeds

12 fresh curry leaves or 1 tbsp dried

6 shallots, finely chopped

1 garlic clove, crushed

1 tsp ground turmeric

½ cup ground coriander

¼–½ tsp chili powder

scant 3 cups coconut cream

1 lb 2 oz/500 g skinless, boneless white fish, such as monkfish or cod, cut into large chunks

1 lb/450 g large raw shrimp, peeled and deveined

juice and finely grated rind of 1 lime

salt

lime slices, to serve

Heat the oil in a kadhai, wok, or large skillet over high heat. Add the mustard seeds and stir them around for about 1 minute, or until they pop. Stir in the curry leaves.

Add the shallots and garlic and stir for about 5 minutes, or until the shallots are golden. Stir in the turmeric, coriander, and chili powder and continue stirring for about 30 seconds.

Add the coconut cream. Bring to a boil, then reduce the heat to medium and stir for about 2 minutes.

Reduce the heat to low, add the fish, and simmer for 1 minute, spooning the sauce over the fish and very gently spooning it around. Add the shrimp and continue to simmer for an additional 4–5 minutes until the fish flakes easily and the shrimp turn pink and curl.

Add half the lime juice, then taste and add more lime juice and salt to taste. Sprinkle with the lime rind and serve with lime slices.

Bengali-Style Fish

serves 4–8

1 tsp ground turmeric

1 tsp salt

6 tbsp mustard oil

2 lb 4 oz/1 kg monkfish or cod fillet, skinned and cut into pieces

4 fresh green chiles

1 tsp finely chopped fresh ginger

1 tsp crushed garlic

2 onions, finely chopped

2 tomatoes, finely chopped

2 cups water

chopped fresh cilantro, to garnish

Naan, to serve

Mix the turmeric and salt together in a small bowl, then spoon the mixture over the fish pieces.

Heat the mustard oil in a large, heavy-bottom skillet. Add the fish and cook until pale yellow. Remove the fish with a slotted spoon and set aside.

Place the chiles, ginger, garlic, onions, and tomatoes in a mortar and grind with a pestle to make a paste. Alternatively, place the ingredients in a food processor and process until smooth.

Transfer the spice paste to a clean skillet and dry-fry until golden brown.

Remove the skillet from the heat and place the fish pieces in the paste without breaking up the fish. Return the skillet to the heat, add the water, and cook over medium heat for 15–20 minutes. Transfer to a warmed serving dish, garnish with chopped cilantro, and serve with naan.

Balti Fish Curry

serves 4–6

2 lb/900 g thick fish fillets, such as monkfish, cod, or haddock, rinsed and cut into large chunks

2 bay leaves, torn

5 oz/140 g ghee or ⅔ cup vegetable or peanut oil

2 large onions, chopped

½ tbsp salt

⅔ cup water

chopped fresh cilantro, to garnish

for the marinade

½ tbsp Garlic & Ginger Paste

1 fresh green chile, seeded and chopped

1 tsp ground coriander

1 tsp ground cumin

½ tsp ground turmeric

¼–½ tsp chili powder

salt

1 tbsp water

To make the marinade, mix the garlic and ginger paste, green chile, coriander, cumin, turmeric, and chili powder together with salt to taste in a large bowl. Gradually stir in the water to form a thin paste. Add the fish chunks and smear with the marinade. Tuck the bay leaves underneath, cover, and let marinate in the refrigerator for at least 30 minutes, or up to 4 hours.

Remove from the refrigerator 15 minutes in advance of cooking. Melt the ghee in a kadhai, wok, or large skillet over medium-high heat. Add the onions, sprinkle with the salt, and sauté, stirring frequently, for 8 minutes, or until they are very soft and golden.

Gently add the fish, bay leaves, and marinade to the pan and stir in the water. Bring to a boil, then immediately reduce the heat and cook the fish for 4–5 minutes, spooning the sauce over the fish and carefully moving the chunks around, until they are cooked through and flake easily. Adjust the seasoning, if necessary, and sprinkle with cilantro.

Fish Curry

serves 4

juice of 1 lime

4 tbsp Thai fish sauce

2 tbsp Thai soy sauce

1 fresh red chile, seeded and chopped

12 oz/350 g monkfish fillet, cut into cubes

12 oz/350 g salmon fillets, skinned and cut into cubes

1¾ cups coconut milk

3 kaffir lime leaves

1 tbsp Thai Red Curry Paste

1 lemongrass stalk (white part only), finely chopped

2 cups jasmine rice, boiled

4 tbsp chopped fresh cilantro

Combine the lime juice, 2 tablespoons of the fish sauce, and the soy sauce in a shallow, nonmetallic dish. Add the chile and the fish, stir to coat, cover with plastic wrap, and let chill for 1–2 hours, or overnight.

Bring the coconut milk to a boil in a pan and add the lime leaves, curry paste, the remaining fish sauce, and the lemongrass. Let simmer gently for 10–15 minutes.

Add the fish and the marinade and let simmer for 4–5 minutes, until the fish is cooked. Serve hot with boiled rice with chopped cilantro stirred through it.

Mixed Fish & Coconut Curry

serves 4

2 tbsp peanut or vegetable oil

6 scallions, cut into 1-inch/ 2.5-cm lengths

1 large carrot, peeled and cut into thin sticks

2 oz/55 g green beans, trimmed and cut into short lengths

2 tbsp Thai Red Curry Paste

3 cups coconut milk

8 oz/225 g skinned white fish fillet, such as cod, cut into 1-inch/ 2.5-cm cubes

8 oz/225 g squid, cleaned and cut into thick rings

8 oz/225 g large raw shrimp, peeled and deveined

⅓ cup fresh bean sprouts

4 oz/115 g dried rice noodles, cooked and drained

handful of fresh cilantro, chopped

handful of fresh Thai basil leaves, to garnish

Heat the oil in a preheated wok. Add the scallions, carrot, and green beans and stir-fry over medium–high heat for 2–3 minutes, or until starting to soften.

Stir in the curry paste, then add the coconut milk. Bring gently to a boil, stirring occasionally, then reduce the heat and simmer for 2–3 minutes. Add all the seafood and bean sprouts and simmer for 2–3 minutes, or until just cooked through and the shrimp have turned pink.

Stir in the cooked noodles and cilantro and cook for 1 minute. Serve immediately, sprinkled with the basil.

Thai Green Fish Curry

serves 4

2 tbsp vegetable oil

1 garlic clove, chopped

2 tbsp Thai Green Curry Paste

1 small eggplant, diced

4 fl oz/120 ml coconut cream

2 tbsp Thai fish sauce

1 tsp sugar

8 oz/225 g firm white fish, cut into pieces

4 fl oz/120 ml fish stock

2 kaffir lime leaves, shredded finely

about 15 leaves fresh Thai basil

fresh dill sprigs, to garnish

Heat the vegetable oil in a large frying pan or preheated wok over a medium heat until almost smoking. Add the garlic and fry until golden. Add the curry paste and stir-fry a few seconds before adding the aubergine. Stir-fry for about 4–5 minutes until softened.

Add the coconut cream, bring to the boil and stir until the cream thickens and curdles slightly. Add the Thai fish sauce and sugar to the frying pan and stir well.

Add the fish pieces and stock. Simmer for 3–4 minutes, stirring occasionally, until the fish is just tender. Add the lime leaves and basil, then cook for a further 1 minute. Transfer to a large, warmed serving dish and garnish with a few sprigs of fresh dill. Serve immediately.

Cod Curry

serves 4

1 tbsp vegetable oil

1 small onion, chopped

2 garlic cloves, chopped

1-inch/2.5-cm piece of fresh ginger, coarsely chopped

2 large ripe tomatoes, peeled and coarsely chopped

⅔ cup fish stock

1 tbsp medium curry paste

1 tsp ground coriander

14 oz/400 g canned chickpeas, drained and rinsed

1 lb 10 oz/750 g cod fillet, cut into large chunks

4 tbsp chopped fresh cilantro

4 tbsp plain yogurt

salt and pepper

freshly cooked rice, to serve

Heat the oil in a large pan over low heat. Add the onion, garlic, and ginger and cook for 4–5 minutes until softened. Remove from the heat. Put the onion mixture into a food processor or blender with the tomatoes and fish stock and process until smooth.

Return to the pan with the curry paste, ground coriander, and chickpeas. Mix well, then let simmer gently for 15 minutes until thickened.

Add the pieces of fish and return to a simmer. Cook for 5 minutes until the fish is just tender. Remove from the heat and let stand for 2–3 minutes.

Stir in the cilantro and yogurt. Season to taste with salt and pepper and serve with rice.

Noodles with Shrimp & Mushroom Curry

serves 4

1 tbsp vegetable or peanut oil

3 shallots, chopped

1 fresh red chile, seeded and chopped

1 tbsp Thai Red Curry Paste

1 lemongrass stalk (white part only), finely chopped

8 oz/225 g cooked peeled shrimp

14 oz/400 g canned straw mushrooms, drained

2 tbsp Thai fish sauce

2 tbsp Thai soy sauce

8 oz/225 g fresh egg noodles

chopped fresh cilantro, to garnish

Heat the oil in a wok and stir-fry the shallots and chile for 2–3 minutes. Add the curry paste and lemongrass and stir-fry for 2–3 minutes.

Add the shrimp, mushrooms, fish sauce, and soy sauce, and stir well to mix.

Meanwhile, cook the noodles in boiling water for 3–4 minutes, drain, and transfer to warmed serving dishes.

Top the noodles with the shrimp curry, sprinkle over the cilantro and serve immediately.

Shrimp Biryani

serves 8

1 tsp saffron strands

4 tbsp lukewarm water

2 shallots, coarsely chopped

3 garlic cloves, crushed

1-inch/2.5-cm piece fresh
ginger, chopped

2 tsp coriander seeds

½ tsp black peppercorns

2 cloves

seeds from 2 green
cardamom pods

1-inch/2.5-cm piece
cinnamon stick

1 tsp ground turmeric

1 green chile, chopped

½ tsp salt

2 tbsp ghee

1 tsp black mustard seeds

1 lb 2 oz/500 g raw jumbo
shrimp in their shells, or
14 oz/400 g raw, peeled
and deveined

1¼ cups coconut milk

1¼ cups lowfat plain yogurt

freshly cooked rice, to serve

to garnish

toasted flaked almonds

1 scallion, sliced

sprigs of fresh cilantro

Soak the saffron in the lukewarm water for 10 minutes. Put the shallots, garlic, ginger, coriander seeds, peppercorns, cloves, cardamom seeds, cinnamon stick, turmeric, chile, and salt into a spice grinder or mortar and grind to a paste.

Heat the ghee in a saucepan and add the mustard seeds. When they start to pop, add the shrimp and stir over a high heat for 1 minute. Stir in the spice mix, then the coconut milk and yogurt. Simmer for 20 minutes.

Spoon the shrimp mixture into warmed serving dishes. Top with the freshly cooked rice and drizzle over the saffron water. Serve garnished with the almonds, scallion, and sprigs of cilantro.

Shrimp Masala

serves 4

2 fresh red chiles, seeded and chopped

2 garlic cloves, chopped

1/2 onion, chopped

1-inch/2.5-cm piece fresh ginger, chopped

1 tsp ground turmeric

1 tsp ground cumin

1 tsp garam masala

1/2 tsp sugar

1/2 tsp pepper

1 1/4 cups plain yogurt

2 tbsp chopped fresh cilantro

1 lb/450 g raw large shrimp, peeled, deveined and tails left intact

lime wedges, to serve

If you are using wooden skewers, soak them in cold water for 30 minutes.

Put the chiles into a food processor with the garlic, onion, ginger, turmeric, cumin, garam masala, sugar, pepper, and yogurt. Process until smooth, then transfer to a large, shallow dish. Stir in the cilantro. Thread the shrimp onto metal kabob skewers or pre-soaked wooden skewers, leaving a small space at either end. Transfer them to the dish and turn in the mixture until thoroughly coated. Cover with plastic wrap and refrigerate for 1–1 1/2 hours.

Preheat the broiler. Remove from the refrigerator and arrange the skewers on a broiler rack. Cook under a preheated medium broiler, turning and basting with the marinade, for 4 minutes or until sizzling and cooked through.

Serve hot with lime wedges for squeezing over.

Shrimp in Coconut Milk

serves 4

1 lb 2 oz/500 g raw jumbo shrimp

4 onions

4 tbsp ghee or vegetable oil

1 tsp garam masala

1 tsp ground turmeric

1 cinnamon stick

2 cardamom pods, lightly crushed

½ tsp chili powder

2 whole cloves

2 bay leaves

1¾ cups coconut milk

1 tsp sugar

salt

pilaf rice, to serve

Shell and devein the jumbo shrimp, then set aside until required. Finely chop 2 of the onions and grate the other 2. Heat the ghee in a large, heavy-bottom skillet. Add the garam masala and cook over low heat, stirring constantly, for 1 minute, or until its aroma is released. Add the chopped onions and cook, stirring occasionally, for 10 minutes, or until golden.

Stir in the grated onions, turmeric, cinnamon, cardamom pods, chili powder, cloves, and bay leaves and cook, stirring constantly, for 5 minutes. Stir in half the coconut milk and the sugar and season to taste with salt. Add the shrimp and cook, stirring frequently for 8 minutes, or until they have changed color.

Stir in the remaining coconut milk and bring to a boil. Taste and adjust the seasoning, if necessary, and serve immediately with pilaf rice.

Bengali Cilantro Shrimp

serves 4

4 fresh green chiles, seeded

4 scallions, chopped

3 garlic cloves

1-inch/2.5-cm piece fresh ginger, chopped

2 tsp corn oil

4 tbsp mustard oil or vegetable oil

1 tbsp ground coriander

1 tsp mustard seeds, crushed

¾ cup coconut milk

1 lb 2 oz/500 g raw jumbo shrimp, peeled and deveined

salt

½ cup fresh cilantro, chopped, plus extra leaves to garnish

freshly cooked rice, to serve

lemon halves, to garnish

Shell and devein the jumbo shrimp, then set aside until required. Place the chiles, scallions, garlic, ginger and corn oil in a food processor and process to a smooth paste. Heat the mustard oil in a large, heavy-bottom skillet. Add the spice paste and cook over low heat, stirring constantly, for 2 minutes.

Add the ground coriander, mustard seeds, and coconut milk and bring to a boil, stirring constantly. Reduce the heat and let simmer for 5 minutes.

Stir in the shrimp and let simmer for an additional 6–8 minutes, or until they have changed color. Season with salt to taste, stir in the chopped cilantro, and serve immediately with freshly cooked rice. Garnish with lemon halves and a few cilantro leaves.

Tandoori Shrimp

serves 4

4 tbsp plain yogurt

2 fresh green chiles, seeded and chopped

½ tbsp Garlic & Ginger Paste

seeds from 4 green cardamom pods

2 tsp ground cumin

1 tsp tomato paste

¼ tsp ground turmeric

¼ tsp salt

pinch of chili powder, ideally Kashmiri chili powder

24 raw jumbo shrimp, thawed if frozen, peeled, deveined, and tails left intact

oil, for greasing

Put the yogurt, chiles, and garlic and ginger paste in a small food processor or spice grinder and whiz until a paste forms. Alternatively use a pestle and mortar. Transfer the paste to a large nonmetallic bowl and stir in the cardamom seeds, cumin, tomato paste, turmeric, salt, and chili powder.

Add the shrimp to the bowl and use your hands to make sure they are coated with the yogurt marinade. Cover the bowl with plastic wrap and chill for at least 30 minutes, or up to 4 hours.

When you are ready to cook, heat a large flat tava, griddle, or skillet over high heat until a few drops of water "dance" when they hit the surface. Use crumpled paper towels or a pastry brush to grease the hot pan very lightly with oil.

Use tongs to lift the shrimp out of the marinade, letting the excess drip back into the bowl, then place the shrimp on the griddle and let them cook for 2 minutes. Flip the shrimp over and cook for an additional 1–2 minutes until they turn pink, curl, and are opaque all the way through when you cut one. Serve the shrimp immediately.

Shrimp with Scallions & Straw Mushrooms

serves 4

2 tbsp vegetable or peanut oil

1 bunch of scallions, chopped

2 garlic cloves, finely chopped

1¼ cups coconut cream

2 tbsp Thai Red Curry Paste

1 cup fish stock

2 tbsp Thai fish sauce

2 tbsp Thai soy sauce

6 sprigs of fresh Thai basil

14 oz/400 g canned straw mushrooms, drained

12 oz/350 g large cooked peeled shrimp

freshly cooked jasmine rice, to serve

Heat the oil in a wok and stir-fry the scallions and garlic for 2–3 minutes. Add the coconut cream, curry paste, and stock and bring just to a boil.

Stir in the fish sauce and soy sauce, then add the basil, mushrooms, and shrimp. Gradually bring to a boil and serve immediately with freshly cooked jasmine rice.

Shrimp & Pineapple Tikka Kabobs

makes 4

1 tsp cumin seeds

1 tsp coriander seeds

½ tsp fennel seeds

½ tsp yellow mustard seeds

¼ tsp fenugreek seeds

¼ tsp nigella seeds

pinch of chili powder

pinch of salt

2 tbsp lemon or pineapple juice

12 raw jumbo shrimp, peeled, deveined, and tails left intact

12 bite-size wedges of fresh or well-drained canned pineapple

chopped fresh cilantro, to garnish

If you are using wooden skewers for this rather than metal ones, place 4 skewers upright in a tall glass of water to soak for 20 minutes so they do not burn under the broiler.

Dry-fry the cumin, coriander, fennel, mustard, fenugreek, and nigella seeds in a hot skillet over high heat, stirring them around constantly, until you can smell the aroma of the spices. Immediately tip the spices out of the pan so they do not burn.

Put the spices in a spice grinder or mortar, add the chili powder and salt to taste, and grind to a fine powder.

Transfer to a nonmetallic bowl and stir in the lemon or pineapple juice.

Add the shrimp to the bowl and stir them around so they are well coated, then set aside to marinate for 10 minutes. Meanwhile, preheat the broiler to high.

Thread 3 shrimp and 3 pineapple wedges alternately on to each metal or pre-soaked wooden skewer. Broil about 4 inches/10 cm from the heat for 2 minutes on each side, brushing with any leftover marinade, until the shrimp turn pink and are cooked through.

Serve the shrimp and pineapple wedges on a plate with plenty of cilantro sprinkled over.

Vegetable
Dishes

Vegetable Curry

serves 4

1 eggplant

8 oz/225 g turnips

12 oz/350 g new potatoes

8 oz/225 g head of cauliflower

8 oz/225 g button mushrooms

1 large onion

3 carrots

6 tbsp ghee

2 garlic cloves, crushed

4 tsp finely fresh ginger, chopped

1–2 fresh green chiles, seeded and chopped

1 tbsp paprika

2 tsp ground coriander

1 tbsp mild or medium curry powder

scant 2 cups vegetable stock

14 oz/400 g canned chopped tomatoes

1 green bell pepper, seeded and sliced

1 tbsp cornstarch

$^2/_3$ cup coconut milk

2–3 tbsp ground almonds

salt and pepper

fresh cilantro sprigs, to garnish

Cut the eggplant, turnips, and potatoes into ½-inch/1-cm cubes. Divide the cauliflower into small florets. The button mushrooms can be used whole or sliced thickly, if preferred. Slice the onion and carrots.

Heat the ghee in a large pan. Add the onion, turnip, potatoes, and cauliflower and cook over low heat, stirring frequently, for 3 minutes. Add the garlic, ginger, chiles, paprika, ground coriander, and curry powder and cook, stirring, for 1 minute.

Add the stock, tomatoes, eggplant, and mushrooms and season with salt. Cover and simmer, stirring occasionally, for 30 minutes, or until tender. Add the green bell pepper and carrots, cover, and cook for an additional 5 minutes.

Place the cornstarch and coconut milk in a bowl, mix into a smooth paste, and stir into the vegetable mixture. Add the ground almonds and simmer, stirring constantly, for 2 minutes. Taste and adjust the seasoning, adding salt and pepper if necessary. Transfer to warmed serving plates and garnish with sprigs of cilantro.

Chunky Potato & Spinach Curry

serves 4

4 tomatoes

2 tbsp peanut or vegetable oil

2 onions, cut into thick wedges

1-inch/2.5-cm piece fresh ginger, chopped

1 garlic clove, chopped

2 tbsp ground coriander

1 lb/450 g potatoes, cut into chunks

2½ cups vegetable stock

1 tbsp Thai Red Curry Paste

8 oz/225 g spinach leaves

Put the tomatoes in a heatproof bowl and cover with boiling water. Leave for 2–3 minutes, then plunge into cold water and peel off the skins. Cut each tomato into quarters and remove and discard the seeds and central core. Set aside.

Heat the oil in a preheated wok. Add the onions, ginger, and garlic and stir-fry over medium–high heat for 2–3 minutes, or until starting to soften. Add the coriander and potatoes and stir-fry for 2–3 minutes. Add the stock and curry paste and bring to a boil, stirring occasionally. Reduce the heat and simmer gently for 10–15 minutes, or until the potatoes are tender.

Add the spinach and the tomato quarters and cook, stirring, for 1 minute, or until the spinach has wilted. Serve immediately.

Vegetable Korma

serves 4

4 tbsp vegetable oil

2 onions, chopped

2 garlic cloves, chopped

1 fresh red chile, chopped

1 tbsp grated fresh ginger, chopped

2 tomatoes, peeled and chopped

1 orange bell pepper, seeded and cut into small pieces

1 large potato, cut into chunks

1¾ cups cauliflower florets

½ tsp salt

1 tsp ground turmeric

1 tsp ground cumin

1 tsp ground coriander

1 tsp garam masala

¾ cups vegetable stock or water

⅔ cups plain yogurt

⅔ cups light cream

1 oz/25 g fresh cilantro, chopped

freshly cooked rice, to serve

Heat the oil in a large pan over medium heat, add the onions and garlic, and cook, stirring, for 3 minutes. Add the chile and ginger and cook for a further 4 minutes. Add the tomatoes, bell pepper, potato, cauliflower, salt, and spices and cook, stirring, for a further 3 minutes. Stir in the stock and bring to a boil. Reduce the heat and simmer for 25 minutes.

Stir in the yogurt and cream and cook, stirring, for an additional 5 minutes. Add the cilantro and heat through.

Serve with freshly cooked rice.

Carrot & Pumpkin Curry

serves 4

⅔ cup vegetable stock

1-inch piece fresh galangal, sliced

2 garlic cloves, chopped

1 lemongrass stalk (white part only), finely chopped

2 fresh red chiles, seeded and chopped

4 carrots, peeled and cut into chunks

8 oz pumpkin, peeled, seeded, and cut into cubes

2 tbsp vegetable or peanut oil

2 shallots, finely chopped

3 tbsp Thai Yellow Curry Paste

1¾ cups coconut milk

4–6 sprigs of fresh Thai basil

⅛ cup toasted pumpkin seeds, to garnish

Pour the stock into a large pan and bring to a boil. Add the galangal, half the garlic, the lemongrass, and chiles, and let simmer for 5 minutes. Add the carrots and pumpkin and let simmer for 5–6 minutes, until tender.

Meanwhile, heat the oil in a wok or skillet and stir-fry the shallots and the remaining garlic for 2–3 minutes. Add the curry paste and stir-fry for 1–2 minutes.

Stir the shallot mixture into the pan and add the coconut milk and Thai basil. Let simmer for 2–3 minutes. Serve hot, sprinkled with the toasted pumpkin seeds.

Chili-Yogurt Mushrooms

serves 4–6

4 tbsp ghee or vegetable or peanut oil

2 large onions, chopped

4 large garlic cloves, crushed

14 oz/400 g canned chopped tomatoes

1 tsp ground turmeric

1 tsp garam masala

½ tsp chili powder

1 lb 10 oz/750 g cremini mushrooms, thickly sliced

pinch of sugar

½ cup plain yogurt

salt and pepper

chopped fresh cilantro, to garnish

freshly cooked rice, to serve

Heat the ghee in a wok, or large skillet over medium–high heat. Add the onions and sauté, stirring frequently, for 5–8 minutes until golden. Stir in the garlic and sauté for an additional 2 minutes.

Add the tomatoes and mix around. Stir in the turmeric, garam masala, and chili powder and continue cooking for an additional 3 minutes.

Add the mushrooms, sugar, and salt to taste and cook for about 8 minutes, until the mushrooms have given off their liquid and are soft and tender.

Turn off the heat, then stir in the yogurt, a little at a time, beating vigorously to prevent it curdling. Taste and adjust the seasoning if necessary. Sprinkle with cilantro and serve with freshly cooked rice.

Butternut Squash Curry

serves 4

2 tbsp peanut or vegetable
oil

1 tsp cumin seeds

2 red onions, sliced

2 celery stalks, sliced

1 large butternut squash,
peeled, seeded, and cut
into chunks

2 tbsp Thai Green Curry
Paste

1¼ cups vegetable stock

2 fresh kaffir lime leaves

⅓ cup fresh bean sprouts

handful of fresh cilantro,
chopped, to garnish

freshly cooked rice,
to serve

Heat the oil in a preheated wok, then add the cumin seeds and stir-fry over medium–high heat for 2–3 minutes, or until starting to pop. Add the onions and celery and stir-fry for 2–3 minutes. Add the squash and stir-fry for 3–4 minutes. Add the curry paste, stock, and lime leaves and bring to a boil, stirring occasionally.

Reduce the heat and simmer gently for 3–4 minutes, or until the squash is tender. Add the bean sprouts and cook for an additional 1–2 minutes, or until hot but still crunchy. Sprinkle the cilantro over the curry and serve with freshly cooked rice.

Pumpkin Curry

serves 4

⅔ cup vegetable oil

2 onions, sliced

½ tsp white cumin seeds

1 lb/450 g pumpkin, cubed

1 tsp aamchoor (dried mango powder)

1 tsp fresh ginger, chopped

1 tsp crushed fresh garlic

1 tsp crushed red chile

½ tsp salt

1¼ cups water

Chapatis, to serve

Heat the oil in a large, heavy-bottom skillet. Add the onions and cumin seeds and cook, stirring occasionally, for 5–6 minutes, until a light golden brown color.

Add the pumpkin to the skillet and stir-fry for 3–5 minutes over low heat.

Mix the aamchoor, ginger, garlic, chile, and salt together in a bowl. Add to the onion and pumpkin mixture in the pan and stir well.

Add the water, cover, and cook over low heat for 10–15 minutes, stirring occasionally. Transfer the curry to warmed serving dishes and serve hot with chapatis.

Eggplant & Bean Curry

serves 4

2 tbsp vegetable or peanut oil

1 onion, chopped

2 garlic cloves, crushed

2 fresh red chiles, seeded and chopped

1 tbsp Thai Red Curry Paste

1 large eggplant, cut into chunks

4 oz/115 g baby eggplants

generous 1 cup baby fava beans

4 oz/115 g fine green beans

1½ cups coconut cream

1 tsp vegetable bouillon powder

3 tbsp Thai soy sauce

1 tsp jaggery or soft light brown sugar

3 kaffir lime leaves, torn coarsely

4 tbsp chopped fresh cilantro

Heat the oil in a wok or large skillet and sauté the onion, garlic, and chiles for 1–2 minutes. Stir in the curry paste and cook for 1–2 minutes.

Add the eggplants and cook for 3–4 minutes, until starting to soften. (You may need to add a little more oil as eggplants soak it up quickly.) Add all the beans and stir-fry for 2 minutes.

Pour in the coconut cream and stir in the bouillon powder, soy sauce, jaggery, and lime leaves. Bring gently to a boil, reduce the heat, and simmer for 5 minutes. Stir in the cilantro and serve hot.

Cauliflower & Sweet Potato Curry

serves 4

4 tbsp ghee or vegetable oil

2 onions, finely chopped

1 tsp Bengali five-spice mix

1 head of cauliflower, broken into florets

12 oz/350 g sweet potatoes, diced

2 fresh green chiles, seeded and finely chopped

1 tsp ginger paste

2 tsp paprika

1½ tsp ground cumin

1 tsp ground turmeric

½ tsp chili powder

3 tomatoes, quartered

2 cups fresh or frozen peas

3 tbsp plain yogurt

1 cup vegetable stock or water

1 tsp garam masala

salt

sprigs of fresh cilantro, to garnish

Heat the ghee in a large, heavy-bottom skillet. Add the onions and Bengali five-spice mix and cook over low heat, stirring frequently, for 10 minutes, or until the onions are golden. Add the cauliflower, sweet potatoes, and chiles and cook, stirring frequently, for 3 minutes.

Stir in the ginger paste, paprika, cumin, turmeric, and chili powder and cook, stirring constantly, for 3 minutes. Add the tomatoes and peas and stir in the yogurt and stock. Season with salt to taste, cover, and let simmer for 20 minutes, or until the vegetables are tender.

Sprinkle the garam masala over the curry, transfer to a warmed serving dish and serve immediately, garnished with sprigs of cilantro.

Zucchini & Cashew Curry

serves 4

2 tbsp vegetable or peanut oil

6 scallions, chopped

2 garlic cloves, chopped

2 fresh green chiles, seeded and chopped

1 lb zucchini, cut into thick slices

4 oz/115 g shiitake mushrooms, halved

½ cup bean sprouts

½ cup cashews, toasted or dry-fried

a few Chinese chives, snipped

4 tbsp Thai soy sauce

1 tsp Thai fish sauce

freshly cooked noodles, to serve

Heat the oil in a wok or large skillet and sauté the scallions, garlic, and chiles for 1–2 minutes, until softened but not browned.

Add the zucchini and mushrooms and cook for 2–3 minutes until tender.

Add the bean sprouts, cashew nuts, chives, soy sauce and fish sauce and stir-fry for 1–2 minutes.

Serve hot with freshly cooked noodles.

Vegetables with Tofu & Spinach

serves 4

vegetable or peanut oil,
for deep-frying

8 oz/225 g firm tofu,
drained and cut into
cubes

2 tbsp vegetable or peanut
oil

2 onions, chopped

2 garlic cloves, chopped

1 fresh red chile, seeded
and sliced

3 celery stalks, diagonally
sliced

8 oz/225 g mushrooms,
thickly sliced

4 oz/115 g baby corn, cut
in half

1 red bell pepper, seeded
and cut into strips

3 tbsp Thai Red Curry Paste

1¾ cups coconut milk

1 tsp jaggery or soft light
brown sugar

2 tbsp Thai soy sauce

5 cups baby spinach leaves

Heat the oil for deep-frying in a skillet and deep-fry the tofu cubes, in batches, for 4–5 minutes, until crisp and browned. Remove with a slotted spoon and drain on paper towels.

Heat 2 tablespoons of the oil in a skillet and stir-fry the onions, garlic, and chile for 1–2 minutes, until they start to soften. Add the celery, mushrooms, corn, and red bell pepper, and stir-fry for 3–4 minutes, until they soften.

Stir in the curry paste and coconut milk and gradually bring to a boil. Add the jaggery and soy sauce and then the spinach. Cook, stirring constantly, until the spinach has wilted. Serve immediately, topped with the tofu.

Eggplant Curry

serves 2

peanut or vegetable oil,
for deep-frying

2 eggplants, cut into
3/4-inch/2-cm cubes

1 bunch of scallions,
coarsely chopped

2 garlic cloves, chopped

2 red bell peppers, seeded
and cut into 3/4-inch/
2-cm squares

3 zucchini, thickly sliced

1¾ cups canned coconut
milk

2 tbsp Thai Red Curry Paste

large handful of fresh
cilantro, chopped, plus
extra sprigs to garnish

Heat the oil for deep-frying in a preheated wok or a deep pan or deep-fat fryer to 350°F/180°C, or until a cube of bread browns in 30 seconds. Add the eggplant cubes, in batches, and cook for 45 seconds–1 minute, or until crisp and brown all over. Remove with a slotted spoon and drain on paper towels.

Heat 2 tablespoons of the oil in a separate preheated wok or large skillet. Add the scallions and garlic and stir-fry over medium high heat for 1 minute. Add the red bell peppers and zucchini and stir-fry for 2–3 minutes. Add the coconut milk and curry paste and bring gently to a boil, stirring occasionally. Add the eggplants and chopped cilantro, then reduce the heat and simmer for 2–3 minutes.

Garnish with sprigs of cilantro and serve immediately.

Green Bean & Potato Curry

serves 6

1¼ cups vegetable oil

1 tsp white cumin seeds

1 tsp mixed mustard and onion seeds

4 dried red chiles

3 fresh tomatoes, sliced

1 tsp salt

1 tsp finely fresh ginger, chopped

1 tsp crushed fresh garlic

1 tsp chili powder

7 oz/200 g green beans, diagonally sliced into 1-inch/2.5-cm pieces

2 potatoes, peeled and diced

1¼ cups water

to garnish

chopped fresh cilantro and green chiles, finely sliced, to garnish

Heat the oil in a large, heavy-bottom pan. Add the white cumin seeds, mustard and onion seeds, and dried red chiles, stirring well.

Add the tomatoes to the pan and stir-fry the mixture for 3–5 minutes.

Mix the salt, ginger, garlic, and chili powder together in a bowl and spoon into the saucepan. Blend the whole mixture together.

Add the green beans and potatoes to the pan and stir-fry for 5 minutes.

Add the water to the pan, reduce the heat, and let simmer for 10–15 minutes, stirring occasionally. Transfer to a warmed serving dish, garnish with chopped cilantro and green chiles and serve.

Okra Curry

serves 4

1 lb/450 g okra

⅔ cup vegetable oil

2 onions, sliced

3 fresh green chiles, finely chopped

2 curry leaves

1 tsp salt

1 tomato, sliced

2 tbsp lemon juice

2 tbsp chopped fresh cilantro

Chapatis, to serve

Rinse the okra and drain thoroughly. Using a sharp knife, chop and discard the ends of the okra. Cut the okra into 1-inch/2.5-cm pieces.

Heat the oil in a heavy-bottom skillet. Add the onions, green chiles, curry leaves, and salt and stir-fry for 5 minutes.

Gradually add the okra, mixing in gently with a slotted spoon, then stir-fry over medium heat for 12–15 minutes.

Add the sliced tomato to the skillet and sprinkle over the lemon juice sparingly.

Sprinkle with chopped cilantro, cover, and let simmer for 3–5 minutes. Transfer to warmed serving plates and serve hot with chapatis.

Chickpea Curry

serves 4

6 tbsp vegetable oil

2 onions, sliced

1 tsp finely fresh ginger, chopped

1 tsp ground cumin

1 tsp ground coriander

1 tsp crushed fresh garlic

1 tsp chili powder

2 fresh green chiles, finely chopped

2–3 tbsp fresh cilantro leaves

2/3 cup water

1 large potato

14 oz/400 g canned chickpeas, drained

1 tbsp lemon juice

Heat the oil in a large, heavy-bottom pan. Add the onions and cook, stirring occasionally, until golden. Reduce the heat, add the ginger, ground cumin, ground coriander, garlic, chili powder, green chiles, and cilantro leaves and stir-fry for 2 minutes.

Add the water to the mixture in the pan and stir to mix.

Using a sharp knife, cut the potato into dice, then add with the chickpeas to the pan. Cover and let simmer, stirring occasionally, for 5–7 minutes.

Sprinkle the lemon juice over the curry. Transfer to warmed serving dishes and serve hot.

Potato & Bell Pepper Curry

serves 4

3 tbsp ghee or vegetable oil

1 onion, chopped

2 potatoes, cut into large chunks

1 tsp chili powder

1 tsp ground coriander

1/4 tsp ground turmeric

2 green bell peppers, seeded and cubed

8 oz/225 g fresh or frozen fava beans

7 oz/200 g canned tomatoes

2 fresh green chiles, coarsely chopped

1 tbsp chopped fresh cilantro

1/2 cup vegetable stock or water

salt

Naan, to serve

Heat the ghee in a large, heavy-bottom pan. Add the onion and cook over low heat, stirring occasionally, for 5 minutes, or until softened. Add the potatoes and cook, stirring occasionally, for 5 minutes.

Add the chili powder, ground coriander, and turmeric and stir well, then add the green bell peppers, fava beans, and the tomatoes and their can juices, breaking up the tomatoes slightly with a wooden spoon.

Stir in the chiles and chopped cilantro, pour in the stock and season to taste with salt. Cover and let simmer for 8–10 minutes, or until the potatoes are tender. Serve immediately with naan.

Zucchini Curry

serves 4

6 tbsp vegetable oil

1 medium onion, finely chopped

3 fresh green chiles, finely chopped

1 tsp fresh ginger, finely chopped

1 tsp crushed fresh garlic

1 tsp chili powder

1 lb 2 oz/500 g zucchini, thinly sliced

2 tomatoes, sliced

2 tsp fenugreek seeds

Chapatis, to serve

Heat the oil in a large, heavy-based skillet. Add the onion, green chiles, ginger, garlic and chili powder to the pan, stirring well to combine.

Add the sliced zucchini and tomatoes to the pan and stir-fry over a medium heat, for 5–7 minutes.

Add the fenugreek seeds to the zucchini mixture in the pan and stir-fry over a medium heat for a further 5 minutes, until the vegetables are tender.

Remove the pan from the heat and transfer to warmed serving dishes. Serve hot with chapatis.

Egg & Lentil Curry

serves 4

3 tbsp ghee or vegetable oil

1 large onion, chopped

2 garlic cloves, chopped

1-inch/2.5-cm piece fresh ginger, chopped

½ tsp minced chile or chili powder

1 tsp ground coriander

1 tsp ground cumin

1 tsp paprika

⅓ cup split red lentils

1¾ cups vegetable stock

8 oz/225 g canned chopped tomatoes

6 eggs

¼ cup coconut milk

salt

2 tomatoes, cut into wedges, and cilantro sprigs, to garnish

Chapatis or Naan, to serve

Heat the ghee in a saucepan, add the onion and fry gently for 3 minutes. Stir in the garlic, ginger, chile and spices and cook gently, stirring frequently, for 1 minute. Stir in the lentils, stock, and tomatoes and bring to the boil. Reduce the heat, cover and simmer, stirring occasionally, for 30 minutes, until the lentils are tender.

Meanwhile, place the eggs in a saucepan of cold water and bring to the boil. Reduce the heat and simmer for 10 minutes. Drain and cover immediately with cold water.

Stir the coconut milk into the lentil mixture and season well with salt. Process the mixture in a blender or food processor until smooth. Return to the pan and heat through.

Shell the hard-cooked eggs and cut in half lengthways. Arrange 3 halves on each serving plate. Spoon the hot lentil sauce over the eggs, adding enough to flood the plate. Arrange a tomato wedge and a cilantro sprig between each halved egg. Serve hot with chapatis or naan.

4

Accompaniments

Onion Bhaji

makes 12

1 cup besan or chickpea flour

1 tsp salt

1 tsp ground cumin

1 tsp ground turmeric

1 tsp baking soda

½ tsp chili powder

2 tsp lemon juice

2 tbsp vegetable or peanut oil, plus extra for deep-frying

2–8 tbsp water

2 onions, thinly sliced

2 tsp coriander seeds, lightly crushed

Sift the besan flour, salt, cumin, turmeric, baking soda, and chili powder into a large bowl. Add the lemon juice and the oil, then very gradually stir in just enough water until a batter similar in consistency to light cream forms. Mix in the onions and coriander seeds.

Heat enough oil for deep-frying in a wok, deep-fat fryer, or large, heavy-bottom pan until it reaches 350°F/180°C, or until a cube of bread browns in 30 seconds. Without overcrowding the pan, drop in spoonfuls of the onion mixture and cook for 2 minutes, then use tongs to flip the bhajis over and cook for an additional 2 minutes, or until golden brown.

Immediately remove the bhajis from the oil and drain well on crumpled paper towels. Keep the bhajis warm while you continue cooking the remaining batter. Serve hot.

Naan

makes 10

6½ cups strong white flour

1 tbsp baking powder

1 tsp sugar

1 tsp salt

1¼ cups water, heated to 122°F/50°C

1 egg, beaten

4 tbsp ghee, melted, plus a little extra for rolling out and brushing

Sift the flour, baking powder, sugar, and salt into a large mixing bowl and make a well in the center. Mix together the water and egg, beating until the egg breaks up and is blended with the liquid.

Slowly add the liquid mixture to the dry ingredients, using your fingers to draw in the flour from the sides, until a stiff, heavy dough forms. Shape the dough into a ball and return it to the bowl.

Soak a clean dish towel in hot water, then wring it out and use it to cover the bowl, tucking the ends of the dish towel under the bowl. Set the bowl aside to let the dough rest for 30 minutes.

Turn out the dough onto a counter brushed with a little melted ghee and flatten the dough. Gradually sprinkle the dough with the melted ghee and knead to work it in, little by little, until it is completely incorporated. Shape the dough into 10 equal balls.

Resoak the dish towel in hot water and wring it out again, then place it over the dough balls and let rest and rise for 1 hour.

Meanwhile, put 1 or 2 cookie sheets in the oven and preheat the oven to 450°F/230°C or its highest setting.

Use a lightly greased rolling pin to roll the dough balls into teardrop shapes, about ⅛ inch/3 mm thick. Use crumpled paper towels to lightly rub the hot cookie sheets with ghee. Arrange the naans on the cookie sheets and bake for 5–6 minutes until they are golden brown and lightly puffed. As you take the naans out of the oven, brush with melted ghee and serve at once.

Vegetarian Samosas

makes 12

2 tbsp vegetable oil

1 onion, chopped

½ tsp ground coriander

½ tsp ground cumin

pinch of ground turmeric

½ tsp ground ginger

½ tsp garam masala

1 garlic clove, crushed

1½ cups diced potatoes

1 cup frozen peas, thawed

5½ oz/150 g spinach, chopped

lime wedges, to garnish

pastry

12 oz/350 g filo pastry

vegetable oil, for deep-frying

To make the filling, heat the oil in a skillet. Add the onion and sauté, stirring frequently, for 1–2 minutes, until softened. Stir in all of the spices and garlic and cook for 1 minute.

Add the potatoes and cook over low heat, stirring frequently, for 5 minutes, until they begin to soften.

Stir in the peas and spinach and cook for 3–4 minutes more.

Lay the filo pastry sheets out on a clean counter and fold 12 sheets in half lengthwise.

Place 2 tablespoons of the vegetable filling at one end of a folded pastry sheet. Fold over one corner to make a triangle. Continue folding in this way to make a triangular package and seal the edges securely with water.

Repeat with the remaining pastry and the remaining filling.

Heat the oil for deep-frying to 350°F/180°C or until a cube of bread browns in 30 seconds. Fry the samosas, in batches, for 1–2 minutes until golden. Drain on absorbent paper towels and keep warm while you are cooking the remainder. Garnish with lime wedges and serve.

Chapatis

makes 6

1½ cups whole wheat flour, sifted, plus extra for dusting

½ tsp salt

⅔–¾ cup water

melted ghee, for brushing

Mix the flour and salt together in a large bowl and make a well in the center. Gradually stir in enough of the water to make a stiff dough.

Turn out the dough onto a lightly floured counter and knead for 10 minutes, or until it is smooth and elastic. Shape the dough into a ball and place it in the cleaned bowl, then cover with a damp dish towel and let rest for 20 minutes.

Divide the dough into 6 equal pieces. Lightly flour your hands and roll each piece of dough into a ball. Meanwhile, heat a large, ungreased, skillet or griddle over high heat until very hot and a splash of water "dances" when it hits the surface.

Working with 1 ball of dough at a time, flatten the dough between your palms, then roll it out on a lightly floured counter into a 7-inch/18-cm circle. Slap the dough onto the hot pan and cook until brown flecks appear on the bottom. Flip the dough over and repeat on the other side.

Flip the dough over again and use a bunched-up dish towel to press down all around the edge. This pushes the steam in the chapati around, causing the chapati to puff up. Continue cooking until the bottom is golden brown, then flip over and repeat this step on the other side.

Brush the chapati with melted ghee and serve, then repeat with the remaining dough balls. Chapatis are best served immediately, as soon as they come out of the pan, but they can be kept warm wrapped in foil for about 20 minutes.

Spiced Potatoes & Spinach

serves 4

1 lb 2 oz/500 g fresh spinach leaves

2 tbsp ghee or vegetable oil

1 tsp black mustard seeds

1 onion, halved and sliced

2 tsp Garlic and Ginger Paste

2 lb/900 g waxy potatoes, cut into small chunks

1 tsp chili powder

½ cup vegetable stock or water

salt

Bring a large pan of water to a boil. Add the spinach leaves and blanch for 4 minutes. Drain well, then tip into a clean dish towel, roll up, and squeeze out the excess liquid.

Heat the ghee in a separate pan. Add the mustard seeds and cook over low heat, stirring constantly, for 2 minutes, or until they give off their aroma. Add the onion and garlic and ginger paste and cook, stirring frequently, for 5 minutes, or until softened.

Add the potatoes, chili powder and stock, and season to taste with salt. Bring to a boil, cover, and cook for 10 minutes.

Add the spinach and stir it in, then cover and let simmer for an additional 10 minutes, or until the potatoes are tender. Serve immediately.

Aloo Gob

serves 4–6

4 tbsp ghee or vegetable or peanut oil

½ tbsp cumin seeds

1 onion, chopped

1½-inch/4-cm piece fresh ginger, finely chopped

1 fresh green chile, seeded and thinly sliced

1 lb/450 g head of cauliflower, cut into small florets

1 lb/450 g large waxy potatoes, peeled and cut into large chunks

½ tsp ground coriander

½ tsp garam masala

¼ tsp salt

fresh cilantro sprigs, to garnish

Heat the ghee in a flameproof casserole or large skillet with a tight-fitting lid over medium–high heat. Add the cumin seeds and stir around for about 30 seconds until they crackle and start to brown.

Immediately stir in the onion, ginger, and chile and stir for 5–8 minutes until the onion is golden.

Stir in the cauliflower and potatoes, followed by the ground coriander, garam masala, and salt and continue stirring for about 30 seconds longer.

Cover the pan, reduce the heat to the lowest setting, and simmer, stirring occasionally, for 20–30 minutes until the vegetables are tender when pierced with the point of a knife. Check occasionally that they aren't sticking to the bottom of the pan and stir in a little water, if necessary.

Serve garnished with sprigs of cilantro.

Matar Paneer

serves 4

3 oz/85 g ghee or 6 tbsp vegetable or peanut oil

12 oz/350 g paneer, cut into ½-inch/1-cm pieces

2 large garlic cloves, chopped

½-inch/1-cm piece fresh ginger, finely chopped

1 large onion, finely sliced

1 tsp ground turmeric

1 tsp garam masala

¼–½ tsp chili powder

3 cups frozen peas or 1 lb 5 oz/600 g fresh peas, shelled

1 fresh bay leaf

½ tsp salt

½ cup water

chopped fresh cilantro, to garnish

Heat the ghee in a large skillet or flameproof casserole with a tight-fitting lid over medium-high heat. Add as many paneer pieces as will fit in a single layer without overcrowding the pan and pan-fry for about 5 minutes until golden brown on all sides. Use a slotted spoon to remove the paneer and drain on crumpled paper towels. Continue, adding a little extra ghee, if necessary, until all the paneer is cooked.

Stir in the garlic, ginger, and onion and sauté, stirring frequently, for 5–8 minutes until the onion is soft, but not brown.

Stir in the turmeric, garam masala, and chili powder and sauté for an additional 2 minutes.

Add the peas, bay leaf, and salt to the pan and stir around. Pour in the water and bring to a boil. Reduce the heat to very low, then cover and simmer for 10 minutes, or until the peas are tender.

Gently return the paneer to the pan. Simmer, stirring gently, until the paneer is heated through. Sprinkle with cilantro and serve.

Coconut Rice

serves 4–6

scant 1¼ cups basmati rice

2 tbsp mustard oil

2¼ cups coconut cream

1½ tsp salt

toasted flaked coconut,
to garnish

Rinse the basmati rice in several changes of water until the water runs clear, then let soak for 30 minutes. Drain and set aside until ready to cook.

Heat the mustard oil in a large skillet or pan with a lid over high heat until it smokes. Turn off the heat and let the mustard oil cool completely.

When you are ready to cook, reheat the mustard oil over medium–high heat. Add the rice and stir until all the grains are coated in oil. Add the coconut cream and bring to a boil.

Reduce the heat to as low as possible, stir in the salt, and cover the pan tightly. Simmer, without lifting the lid, for 8–10 minutes until the grains are tender and all the liquid is absorbed.

Turn off the heat and use 2 forks to mix the rice. Re-cover the pan and let the rice stand for 5 minutes. Serve garnished with toasted flaked coconut.

Fruit & Nut Pilaf

serves 4–6

scant 1¼ cups basmati rice

2 cups water

½ tsp saffron threads

1 tsp salt

2 tbsp ghee or vegetable or peanut oil

generous ⅓ cup blanched almonds

1 onion, thinly sliced

1 cinnamon stick, broken in half

seeds from 4 green cardamom pods

1 tsp cumin seeds

1 tsp black peppercorns, lightly crushed

2 bay leaves

3 tbsp finely chopped dried mango

3 tbsp finely chopped dried apricots

2 tbsp golden raisins

generous ⅓ cup pistachios, chopped

Rinse the basmati rice in several changes of water until the water runs clear, then let soak for 30 minutes. Drain and set aside until ready to cook.

Boil the water in a small pan. Add the saffron threads and salt, remove from the heat, and set aside to infuse.

Heat the ghee in a large pan with a tight-fitting lid over medium high heat. Add the almonds and stir them around until golden brown, then immediately scoop them out of the pan using a slotted spoon.

Add the onion to the pan and sauté, stirring frequently, for 5–8 minutes until golden, but not brown. Add the spices and bay leaves to the pan and stir them around for about 30 seconds.

Add the rice to the pan and stir until the grains are coated with ghee. Add the saffron-infused water and bring to a boil. Reduce the heat to as low as possible, stir in the dried fruits, and cover the pan tightly. Simmer, without lifting the lid, for 8–10 minutes until the grains are tender and all the liquid is absorbed.

Turn off the heat and use 2 forks to mix the almonds and pistachios into the rice. Re-cover the pan and let stand for 5 minutes before serving.

Spiced Basmati Pilaf

serves 4

2½ cups basmati rice

6 oz/175 g head of broccoli

6 tbsp vegetable oil

2 large onions, chopped

8 oz/225 g button mushrooms, sliced

2 garlic cloves, crushed

6 cardamom pods, split

6 whole cloves

8 black peppercorns

1 cinnamon stick or piece of cassia bark

1 tsp ground turmeric

5 cups boiling vegetable stock or water

⅓ cup seedless raisins

½ cup unsalted pistachios, coarsely chopped

salt and pepper

Place the rice in a strainer and wash well under cold running water. Drain. Trim off most of the broccoli stalk and cut into small florets, then quarter the stalk lengthwise and cut diagonally into 1-cm/½-inch pieces.

Heat the oil in a large pan. Add the onions and broccoli stalks and cook over low heat, stirring frequently, for 3 minutes. Add the mushrooms, rice, garlic, and spices and cook for 1 minute, stirring, until the rice is coated in oil.

Add the boiling stock and season to taste with salt and pepper. Stir in the broccoli florets and return the mixture to a boil. Cover, reduce the heat, and cook over low heat for 15 minutes without uncovering the pan.

Remove the pan from the heat and let the pilaf stand for 5 minutes without uncovering. Remove the whole spices, add the raisins and pistachios, and gently fork through to fluff up the grains. Serve the pilaf hot.

Lemon Rice

serves 4–6

scant 1¼ cups basmati rice

2 tbsp ghee or vegetable or
peanut oil

1 tsp nigella seeds

2 cups water

juice and finely grated rind
of 1 large lemon

1½ tsp salt

¼ tsp ground turmeric

Rinse the basmati rice in several changes of water until the water runs clear, then let soak for 30 minutes. Drain and set aside until ready to cook.

Heat the ghee in a large pan with a tight-fitting lid over medium–high heat. Add the nigella seeds and rice and stir until all the grains are coated in ghee. Add the water and bring to a boil.

Reduce the heat to as low as possible, stir in half the lemon juice, the salt, and turmeric, and cover the pan tightly. Simmer, without lifting the lid, for 8–10 minutes until the grains are tender and all the liquid is absorbed.

Turn off the heat and use 2 forks to mix the lemon rind and remaining juice into the rice. Re-cover the casserole and let the rice stand for 5 minutes before serving.

Plantain Chips

serves 4

4 ripe plantains

1 tsp mild, medium, or hot curry powder, to taste

vegetable or peanut oil, for deep-frying

Mango Chutney, to serve

Peel the plantains, then cut crosswise into 1/8-inch/3-mm slices. Put the slices in a bowl, sprinkle over the curry powder, and use your hands to toss them lightly together.

Heat enough oil for deep-frying in a wok, deep-fat fryer, or large, heavy-bottom pan to 350°F/180°C, or until a cube of bread browns in 30 seconds. Add as many plantain slices as will fit in the pan without overcrowding and cook for 2 minutes, or until golden.

Remove the plantain chips from the pan with a slotted spoon and drain well on crumpled paper towels. Serve hot with mango chutney.

Coconut Sambal

makes about 5 oz/140 g

½ fresh coconut or 1¼ cups dry unsweetened coconut

2 fresh green chiles, seeded or not, to taste, and chopped

1-inch/2.5-cm piece fresh ginger, peeled and finely chopped

4 tbsp chopped fresh cilantro

2 tbsp lemon juice, or to taste

2 shallots, very finely chopped

If you are using a whole coconut, use a hammer and nail to punch a hole in the "eye" of the coconut, then pour out the milk from the inside and reserve. Use the hammer to break the coconut in half, then peel half and chop.

Put the coconut and chiles in a food processor and process for about 30 seconds until finely chopped. Add the ginger, cilantro, and lemon juice and process again.

If the mixture seems too dry, stir in about 1 tablespoon of coconut milk or water. Stir in the shallots and serve immediately, or cover and chill until required. This will keep its fresh flavor in the refrigerator for up to 3 days.

Mango Chutney

makes about 9 oz/250 g

1 large mango, about 14 oz/400 g, peeled, pitted, and finely chopped

2 tbsp lime juice

1 tbsp vegetable or peanut oil

2 shallots, finely chopped

1 garlic clove, finely chopped

2 fresh green chiles, seeded and finely sliced

1 tsp black mustard seeds

1 tsp coriander seeds

5 tbsp grated jaggery or brown sugar

5 tbsp white wine vinegar

1 tsp salt

pinch of ground ginger

Put the mango in a nonmetallic bowl with the lime juice and set aside.

Heat the oil in a large skillet or pan over medium-high heat. Add the shallots and sauté for 3 minutes. Add the garlic and chiles and stir for an additional 2 minutes, or until the shallots are soft, but not brown. Add the mustard and coriander seeds, then stir around.

Add the mango to the pan with the jaggery, vinegar, salt, and ginger and stir around. Reduce the heat to its lowest setting and simmer for 10 minutes until the liquid thickens and the mango becomes sticky.

Remove from the heat and let cool completely. Transfer to an airtight container, cover, and chill for 3 days before using. Store in the refrigerator and use within 1 week.

Raita

serves 4–6

1 large piece cucumber, about 10½ oz/ 300 g, rinsed

1 teaspoon salt

1¾ cups plain yogurt

½ teaspoon sugar

pinch of ground cumin

2 tablespoons chopped fresh cilantro or mint

chili powder, to garnish

Lay a clean dish towel flat on the counter. Coarsely grate the unpeeled cucumber directly onto the dish towel. Sprinkle with ½ teaspoon of the salt, then gather up the dish towel and squeeze until all the excess moisture is removed from the cucumber.

Put the yogurt into a bowl and beat in the remaining ½ teaspoon of salt, along with the sugar and cumin. Stir in the grated cucumber. Taste and add extra seasoning, if you like. Cover and chill until ready to serve.

Stir in the chopped cilantro and transfer to a serving bowl. Sprinkle with chili powder and serve.

Lime Pickle

makes 8 oz/225 g

12 limes, halved and seeded

4 oz/115 g salt

2½ oz/70 g chili powder

1 oz/25 g mustard powder

1 oz/25 g ground fenugreek

1 tbsp ground turmeric

1¼ cups mustard oil

½ oz/15 g yellow mustard seeds, crushed

½ tsp asafetida

Cut each lime half into 4 pieces and pack them into a large sterilized jar, sprinkling over the salt at the same time. Cover and let stand in a warm place for 10–14 days, or until the limes have turned brown and softened.

Mix the chili powder, mustard powder, fenugreek, and turmeric together in a small bowl and add to the jar of limes. Stir to mix, then re-cover and let stand for 2 days.

Transfer the lime mixture to a heatproof bowl. Heat the mustard oil in a heavy-bottom skillet.

Add the mustard seeds and asafetida to the pan and cook, stirring constantly, until the oil is very hot and just starting to smoke. Pour the oil and spices over the limes and mix well. Cover and let cool. When cool, pack into a sterilized jar. Seal and store in a sunny place for 1 week before serving.

Chile & Onion Chutney

makes 8 oz/225 g

1–2 fresh green chiles, seeded or not, to taste, and finely chopped

1 small Thai chile, seeded or not, to taste, and finely chopped

1 tbsp white wine vinegar or cider vinegar

2 onions, finely chopped

2 tbsp fresh lemon juice

1 tbsp sugar

3 tbsp chopped fresh cilantro, mint, or parsley, or a combination of herbs

salt

chile flower, to garnish

Put the chiles in a small nonmetallic bowl with the vinegar, stir around, and then drain. Return the chiles to the bowl and stir in the onions, lemon juice, sugar, and herbs, then add salt to taste.

Let stand at room temperature or cover and chill for 15 minutes. Garnish with the chile flower before serving the chutney.

almonds
  beef korma with almonds 44
  fruit & nut pilaf 143
  lamb pasanda 29
  vegetable curry 88

bean sprouts
  butternut squash curry 99
  fish curry with rice noodles 52
  mixed fish & coconut curry 64
  zucchini & cashew nut curry 106
beef
  balti beef curry 41
  beef dhansak 47
  beef korma with almonds 44
  beef madras 38
  coconut beef curry 42
bell peppers
  balti beef curry 41
  chicken jalfrezi 17
  eggplant curry 111
  potato & bell pepper curry 118
  red curry with pork 35
  vegetable curry 88
  vegetable korma 93
  vegetables with tofu &
    spinach 108
broccoli: spiced basmati pilaf 144
butternut squash curry 99

carrots
  carrot & pumpkin curry 94
  mixed fish & coconut curry 64
  vegetable curry 88
cauliflower
  aloo gob 137
  cauliflower & sweet potato
    curry 105
  vegetable curry 88
  vegetable korma 93
celery
  butternut squash curry 99
  vegetables with tofu &
    spinach 108
chapatis 132
cheese: matar paneer 138
chicken
  balti chicken 20
  chicken jalfrezi 17
  chicken korma 14
  chicken tikka masala 12
  Thai green chicken curry 18
chickpea curry 117
chile & onion chutney 158
coconut milk/cream
  beef madras 38
  Bengali cilantro shrimp 79
  carrot & pumpkin curry 94
  coconut beef curry 42
  coconut rice 140
  egg & lentil curry 123
  eggplant & bean curry 102
  eggplant curry 111
  fish in coconut milk 55
  fish curry 62
  fish curry with rice noodles 52
  Goan Style seafood curry 56
  lamb, tomato & eggplant
    curry 24
  mixed fish & coconut curry 64

mixed seafood curry 50
red curry with pork 35
shrimp biryani 73
shrimp in coconut milk 76
shrimp with scallions & straw
  mushrooms 82
Thai green chicken curry 18
Thai green fish curry 67
vegetable curry 88
vegetables with tofu &
  spinach 108
coconut sambal 150
cod
  balti fish curry 61
  Bengali-style fish 58
  cod curry 68
  fish curry with rice noodles 52
  fish in coconut milk 55
  Goan-style seafood curry 56
  mixed fish & coconut curry 64
corn: vegetables with tofu &
  spinach 108
cucumber: raita 55
curry pastes
  garlic & ginger paste 9
  mussaman curry paste 9
  Thai green curry paste 8
  Thai red curry paste 8
  Thai yellow curry paste 8

egg & lentil curry 123
eggplant
  beef dhansak 47
  eggplant & bean curry 102
  eggplant curry 111
  lamb, tomato & eggplant curry 24
  Thai green chicken curry 18
  Thai green fish curry 67
  vegetable curry 88

fava beans
  chicken jalfrezi 17
  eggplant & bean curry 102
  potato & bell pepper curry 118
fish
  balti fish curry 61
  fish curry with rice noodles 52
  fish in coconut milk 55
  Goan-Style seafood curry 56
  mixed fish & coconut curry 64
  Thai green fish curry 67
  see also individual varieties
fruit & nut pilaf 143

green beans
  eggplant & bean curry 102
  green bean & potato curry 112
  mixed fish & coconut curry 64

haddock
  balti fish curry 61
  fish in coconut milk 55

lamb
  lamb do piaza 26
  lamb pasanda 29
  lamb rogan josh 23
  lamb, tomato & eggplant curry 24
  lean lamb cooked in spinach 30
lentils

beef dhansak 47
egg & lentil curry 123
lime pickle 156

mango chutney 152
matar paneer 138
monkfish
  balti fish curry 61
  Goan-style seafood curry 56
  fish curry 62
  fish curry with rice noodles 52
mushrooms
  chili-yogurt mushrooms 96
  noodles with shrimp &
    mushrooms curry 70
  fish curry with rice noodles 52
  red curry with pork 35
  shrimp with scallions & straw
    mushrooms 82
  spiced basmati pilaf 144
  vegetable curry 88
  vegetables with tofu &
    spinach 108
  zucchini & cashew nut curry 106
mussels: mixed seafood curry 50

naan 128
nuts
  fruit & nut pilaf 143
  spiced basmati pilaf 144
  zucchini & cashew nut curry 106
  see also almonds

okra curry 114
onion bhaji 126

peas
  cauliflower & sweet potato
    curry 105
  matar paneer 138
  vegetarian samosas 131
pineapple: shrimp & pineapple tikka
  kabobs 85
plantain chips 149
pork
  pork with cinnamon &
    fenugreek 32
  pork vindaloo 36
  red curry with pork 35
potatoes
  aloo gob 137
  chunky potato & spinach
    curry 90
  green bean & potato curry 112
  potato & bell pepper curry 118
  spiced potatoes & spinach 134
  vegetable curry 88
  vegetable korma 93
  vegetarian samosas 131
pumpkin
  beef dhansak 47
  carrot & pumpkin curry 94
  pumpkin curry 100

raita 155
rice
  coconut rice 140
  fruit & nut pilaf 143
  lemon rice 146
  spiced basmati pilaf 144

salmon
samosas: vegetables samosas 131
  fish curry 62
  fish curry with rice noodles 52
  mixed seafood curry 50
shrimp
  Bengali cilantro shrimp 79
  noodles with shrimp &
    mushrooms curry 70
  fish in coconut milk 55
  Goan-Style seafood curry 56
  mixed fish & coconut curry 64
  mixed seafood curry 50
  shrimp biryani 73
  shrimp in coconut milk 76
  shrimp masala 74
  shrimp & pineapple tikka
    kabobs 85
  shrimp with scallions & straw
    mushrooms 82
  tandoori shrimp 80
spinach
  chunky potato & spinach
    curry 90
  lean lamb cooked in spinach 30
  spiced potatoes & spinach 134
  vegetables with tofu &
    spinach 108
  vegetarian samosas 131
squid
  fish in coconut milk 55
  mixed fish & coconut curry 64
  mixed seafood curry 50
sweet potatoes: cauliflower & sweet
  potato curry 105

tofu: vegetables with tofu &
  spinach 108
tomatoes
  balti beef curry 41
  balti chicken 20
  Bengali-style fish 58
  cauliflower & sweet potato
    curry 105
  chicken tikka masala 12
  chili-yogurt mushrooms 96
  chunky potato & spinach
    curry 90
  cod curry 68
  egg & lentil curry 123
  green bean & potato curry 112
  lamb rogan josh 23
  lamb, tomato & eggplant
    curry 24
  potato & bell pepper curry 118
  red curry with pork 35
  vegetable curry 88
  vegetable korma 93
  zucchini curry 120
tuna: mixed seafood curry 50
turnips: vegetable curry 88

zucchini
  beef dhansak 47
  eggplant curry 111
  zucchini & cashew nut curry 106
  zucchini curry 120